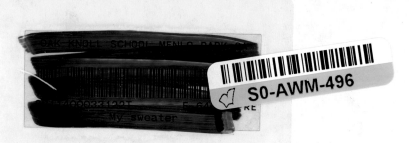

# My Sweater

# For Luke

**For a free color catalog describing Gareth Stevens' list of high-quality books, call 1-800-542-2595 (USA) or 1-800-461-9120 (Canada). Gareth Stevens' Fax: (414) 225-0377.**

**Library of Congress Cataloging-in-Publication Data**

Pressling, Robert.
    My sweater / by Robert Pressling; photographs by Fiona Pragoff.
      p.  cm. — (First step science)
    Includes bibliographical references and index.
    ISBN 0-8368-1187-9
    1. Wool—Juvenile literature.  2. Sweaters—Juvenile literature.  3. Science—Juvenile literature.
  [1. Sweaters.  2. Wool.]  I. Pragoff, Fiona, ill.  II. Title.  III. Series.
  TS1547.P68  1995
  646.4'54—dc20                                      94-34045

This edition first published in 1995 by
**Gareth Stevens Publishing**
1555 North RiverCenter Drive, Suite 201
Milwaukee, Wisconsin 53212, USA

This edition © 1995 by Gareth Stevens, Inc. Original edition published in 1990 by A & C Black (Publishers) Ltd., 35 Bedford Row, London WC1R 4JH. © 1990 A & C Black (Publishers) Ltd. Photographs © 1990 Fiona Pragoff. Additional end matter © 1995 by Gareth Stevens, Inc.

Series editor: Patricia Lantier-Sampon
Editorial assistants: Mary Dykstra, Diane Laska
Illustrations: Alex Ayliffe
Science consultant: Dr. Bryson Gore

Printed in the United States of America
1 2 3 4 5 6 7 8 9 99 98 97 96 95

First Step Science

# My Sweater

by Robert Pressling
photographs by Fiona Pragoff

Gareth Stevens Publishing
**MILWAUKEE**

Look at all the colors
and patterns on these
sweaters. Which one
do you like best?

This is my favorite sweater.

On the label, there is a special picture.
It means my sweater is made from wool.

When I pull on my sweater,
it feels soft and warm.

7

The pattern goes all around my sweater.

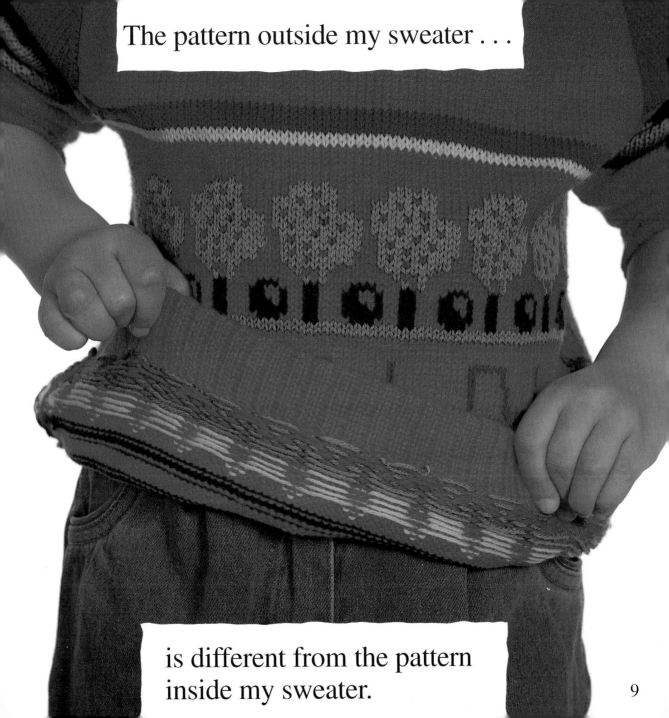

The pattern outside my sweater . . .

is different from the pattern
inside my sweater.

9

My sweater can stretch. If Emily lets go, what will happen?

10

My sweater is full of little holes.
I can see through my sweater.

11

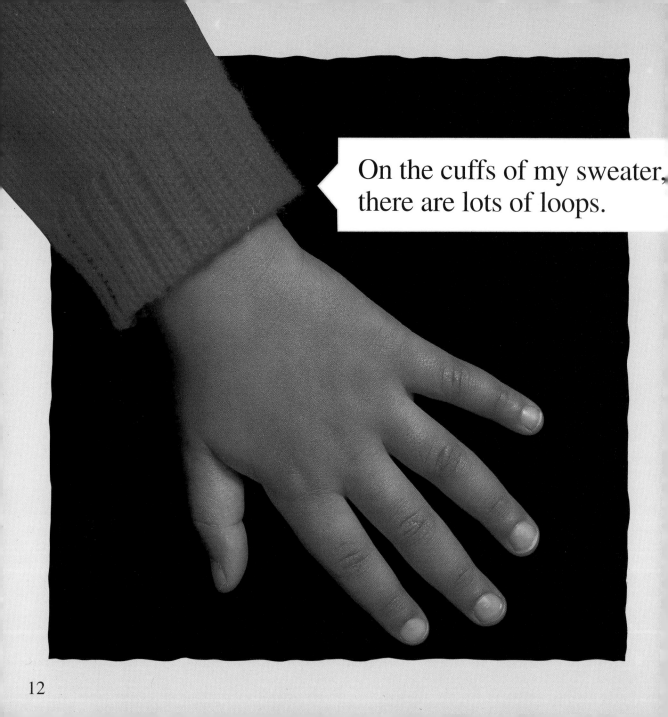

On the cuffs of my sweater, there are lots of loops.

Simon is knitting a sweater.

Can you see how he loops the wool around the needles?

Oops! I've spilled ice cream.
My sweater needs to be washed.

Simon and Emily
are helping me
wash my sweater.

Look at all the bubbles!

17

My sweater soaks
up the water.
It feels heavy.

If I squeeze out the water,
my sweater feels lighter.

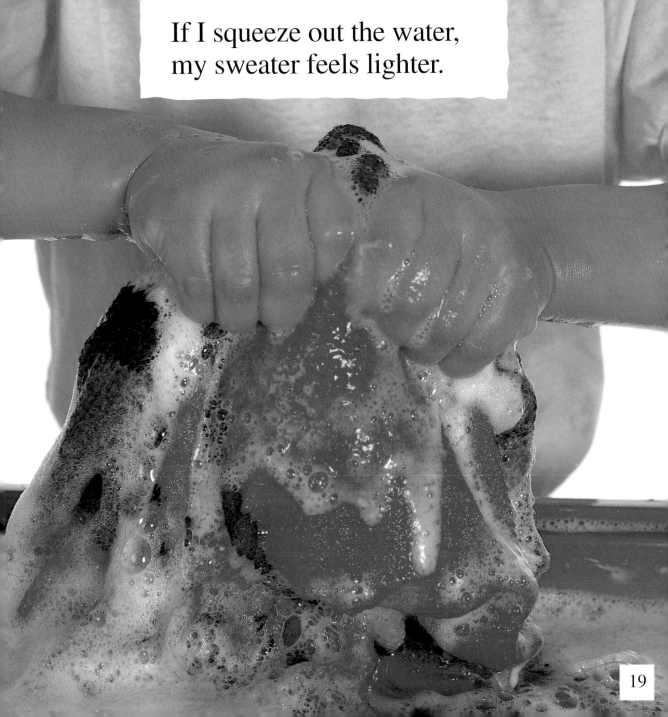

Tomorrow, we are going to a farm.

I'm going to wear my clean sweater.

This wool comes from a sheep.

It looks and feels different from the wool in my sweater.

# FOR MORE INFORMATION

## Notes for Parents and Teachers

**As you share this book with young readers, these notes may help you explain the scientific concepts behind the different activities.**

**pages 4-5, 8, 9**
**Colors and patterns**
Sweaters can be sorted according to color or pattern. Patterns with many colors are made by carrying each color along the back of the sweater and joining it into the knitting each time it is needed.

**page 6  Labels on sweaters**
This is the international symbol for products made from pure new wool. It is called the woolmark. The same symbol is used all over the world.

**page 7  How warm are sweaters?**
Wool traps a dry layer of air that helps hold in body heat and keep us warm. This ability to stop heat escape is called insulation.

**pages 10, 11**
**Stretching sweaters**
Wool fibers are flexible and can be bent and twisted again and again without breaking. A wool fiber can stretch up to 40 percent beyond its original length before it breaks. This makes wool very difficult to tear. The fibers have a natural waviness, called crimp, that makes the fibers spring back into shape after being stretched.

**pages 12, 13  Knitting sweaters**
A good way to see how knitting

works is to find an old woolen sweater and pull it apart to show how the wool is looped together in stitches. The loops on the cuffs of a sweater show where the wool was cast on to make the first row of loops.

## pages 15, 16, 17, 18, 19, 20, 21 Washing sweaters

Soap breaks down the surface tension of the water so it forms smaller droplets and flows into all the places where dirt is trapped. Soap also surrounds the particles of dirt and makes them float off into the water so they can be rinsed away. If the water is too hot, the wool will shrink.

## pages 18, 19 Wet sweaters

On the surface, a wool fiber has overlapping scales (like tiny roof tiles) that repel liquid. But the inner core of the fiber absorbs moisture. So a small amount of water will run off the surface of a woolen sweater. But if the wool gets really wet, it soaks up a lot of water and becomes very heavy.

## pages 22, 23 Wool from sheep

The wool from a sheep has to be processed before it can be used to knit sweaters. It is washed, dyed, carded (untangled), rolled into a sausage shape called a sliver, and finally spun into yarn. See if young readers can find out more about all the different stages in processing wool.

## pages 24, 25 All sorts of wool

The wool in shops comes in different thicknesses, such as four-ply and two-ply. Most wool comes from sheep, but fluffy mohair wool comes from goats, and angora wool comes from rabbits.

# Things to Do

## 1. Wool and other fibers

Wool is a very special kind of fiber. Compare and contrast it to other fibers, such as cotton, silk, and nylon. Look at the fibers with a magnifying glass and closely investigate the weight, feel (texture), stretching ability, and strength of each fiber. How far will each fiber stretch before it breaks? Wool shrinks in hot water. Does this always happen to other fibers? Which fibers are best at keeping things warm or cool?

## 2. Yarn shopping

Visit a fabric, craft, or specialty store that sells yarn and compare the many different kinds and colors of yarn available. Can you tell which yarns are wool and which are not?

## 3. Design a pattern

Design your own pattern for a sweater. Use graph paper and different colored pencils. Each square stands for one stitch. Make a colored cross in each square to show the color you want each stitch to be. You might design a pattern with animals, trains, or a favorite food or toy.

## 4. Mitten vs. mitten

Conduct an experiment with one woolen mitten and one mitten made from acrylic fiber. Sprinkle 3 tablespoons (45 milliliters) of water on the back of each mitten. Then place each mitten wet side down on a paper towel. Does one mitten absorb more water than the other? Does the water slide off one mitten faster than the other?

# Fun Facts about Sweaters and Wool

**1.** Sweaters that are not made of wool are sometimes made of humanmade fibers, such as nylon and acrylic. These fibers are made from oil, coal, and wood.

**2.** It takes about five minutes to shear a sheep using a special clippers called an electric shears.

**3.** The fleece from a sheep must be washed before it is turned into yarn. If it is not washed, a sweater might have a bag of weed seeds and several cups of mud in it!

**4.** Most sweaters purchased in stores are made by knitting machines in large factories. The knitting machines have lots of very small needles and can be programmed to follow a pattern.

**5.** Australia, the world's major wool producer, has over 100 million sheep. These sheep produce enough wool fiber to stretch from Earth to the Sun eight thousand times!

**6.** Felt made from wool is used to cover tennis balls because it is so strong and springy. Felt is a material that is made by pressing wet wool together under pressure.

**7.** The fleece from one sheep has millions of fibers side by side.

**8.** Baseball manufacturers use wool yarn to make baseballs because wool is so strong. The yarn is wrapped tightly around the center of the baseball before it is covered with other materials.

# Glossary

**bubbles** — balls of air or gas surrounded by a thin covering or film of some kind.

**cuff** — the bottom part of a sleeve or pant leg.

**heavy** — weighing a lot.

**knitting** — a type of stitchery using looped yarn and needles to make things like sweaters, mittens, and scarves.

**label** — a tag that gives information.

**light** — not weighing very much.

**loop** — a fold or doubling of a line, ribbon, thread, string, or other material that leaves an opening or an empty space.

**needles** — long metal, plastic, or wooden tools around which yarn is wrapped when knitting.

**pattern** — a design. A pattern can show you a diagram for how something should look or how it should be made.

**pull** — to tug or yank.

**sheep** — a type of animal that has a thick coat of wool. Sheep are raised for food and also for their wool.

**soak** — to make very wet.

**spill** — to cause a substance to overflow or fall out of its container or space.

**stretch** — to reach out in length; to make something longer by pulling the ends.

**wool** — the fine fibers of hair that grow on animals such as sheep; a fabric made from this hair.

## Places to Visit

Everything we do involves some basic scientific principles. Listed below are a few museums that offer a variety of scientific information and experiences. You may also be able to locate other museums in your area. Just remember: you don't always have to visit a museum to experience the wonders of science. Science is everywhere!

Museum of Science and Industry
57th Street and Lake Shore Drive
Chicago, IL  60637

The Smithsonian Institution
1000 Jefferson Drive SW
Washington, D.C.  20560

Royal British Columbia Museum
675 Belleview Street
Victoria, British Columbia
V8V 1X4

San Francisco Craft and Folk
   Art Museum
Bldg. A, Fort Mason Center
San Francisco, CA  94123

Canadian Museum of Carpets
   and Textiles
55 Centre Avenue
Toronto, Ontario  M5G 2H5

## More Books to Read

*Clothes Sticker Activity Book*
   Lara Tankel Holtz
   (Dorling Kindersley)

*Fibers*
   B. J. Knapp
   (Atlantic Europe Publishing)

*From Sheep to Scarf*
  Ali Mitgutsch
  (Carolrhoda)

*Knitting*
  A. Wilkes and C. Garbera
  (Usborne)

*Mr. Nick's Knitting*
  Margaret Wild
  (Harcourt Brace Jovanovich)

*Wool*
  Annabelle Dixon
  (Garrett Educational Corp.)

## Videotapes

*Clothing* (EBE)

*Sheep, Shearing and Spinning:
  A Story of Wool*
    (International Film Bureau)

## Index